Leadership's Future

Confronting Not Condoning!

by

Tom Casey and Claire Hebert-Dow

with

Elizabeth Freudmann and Sean Casey

TELEMACHUS PRESS

Cover designed by Telemachus Press, LLC

Cover art:
Copyright © Color Brush/iStock/44652960

Publishing services by Telemachus Press, LLC
7652 Sawmill Road Suite 304
Dublin, Ohio 43016
http://www.telemachuspress.com

Visit the author website:
http://www.discussionpartners.com

ISBN: 978-1-965121-02-3 (eBook)
ISBN: 978-1-965121-03-0 (Paperback)

Version 2024.08.22

Testimonials

I have worked with Tom Casey since 2021. Few strategic thinkers have been as generous or prolific in stewarding the future of our 44-year old Not-For-Profit as Tom relying on **Discussion Partners** *research and experience. He has led provocative, mission critical strategy discussions with the Associations Board of Directors, on our envisioned future. His previous books on Leadership and Executive Transitions have formed the basis of speeches to our membership.* **Leaderships Future-Confronting Not Condoning!** *is a welcome installation for many reasons. The most important is a needed mirror for much of today's bad behaviors. This book is foundational to improving leadership practices to promote organizational effectiveness and success.*

Robin Antonellis—Executive Director New England
Employee Benefit Council
Former Chief Human Resources Officer Dana-Farber
Cancer Institute

I have worked with Tom Casey and **Discussion Partners** *for several years on leadership development efforts. They are constantly looking over the horizon for trends and themes. As a result through their research, they are able to interpret patterns and undercurrents in leadership that may not yet be apparent to most. With respect to their latest research on objectionable leadership behavior, they have identified key traits including hypocrisy that leaders need to avoid in order to succeed. Both existing and aspiring leaders would do well to heed* **DPC's** *admonitions and prognostications.*

Michael J. Cahalane Esq—Co-Managing Partner
Cetrulo Law LLC

I have known Tom Casey and **Discussion Partners** *for over a decade first as an Advisor and later member of the Board of Directors. Their book,* **Leadership Development-The Next Curve to Flatten!** *profoundly influenced my leadership style through meticulous research and definition of necessary attributes empathy, transparency, accountability & collaboration.* **DPC's** *upcoming book,* **Leadership's Future-Confronting Not Condoning!** *leveraging research from 1800 sources, delves deeper into the nuances of leadership through the identification of undesirable behaviors. I venture the lessons learned are transformative.*

Dr. Joseph Defeo—Principal Juran Institute
Author of *Juran Quality Handbook*

I have known Tom Casey for quite some time, first as a fellow Board Member at **Juran Global** *and most recently as a frequent guest on our Podcast. Today's reality is we are a nation where 50 of us tell Pollsters we prefer a leader who represents overt objectionable behaviors.*

History tells us when a ruthless villain is elevated to a position of power, and their self-indulgent behaviors are perceived as strengths, or ignored, there are unforeseen usually unfavorable outcomes. **Discussion Partner's** *focus on reprehensible behaviors as we and other nations approach elections, is timely, well researched, and their findings persuasive.*

Dr. David Fearon—Professor Emeritus-Central Connecticut
State University
Co-Founder of *Practice?* Podcast
Co-Author with Dr. Peter Vail of *On Practice as A Way of Being*

I have worked with Tom Casey and **Discussion Partners** *for over 20 years and have been a supporter and contributor to a number of their research breakthroughs. Their latest book* **Leadership's Future-Confronting Not Condoning!** *positions societal and work environment opportunities and challenges squarely in our line of sight. We can choose to avoid the obvious or* *embrace the possibilities for the good of our organizations, and ourselves, for professional sanity. Great work on this "in your face" release.*

Greg Flores—Former Chief Human Resources Officer TJX
Companies
Presently Advisor & Board Member

For many years Tom Casey's advice and counsel have been very important in planning for several career transitions. The Transition Advisory services and research provided by Tom and **DPC** *have been invaluable. The newest book* **Leadership's Future-Confronting Not Condoning!** *is a reminder of our obligations and moreover the scrutiny under which our behaviors are judged.*

Steve Krichmar—Independent Trustee of Goldman
Sachs Funds
Former Chief of Operations Putnam Investments &
Partner PwC

The **AllySHIFT** *movement was created as a progressive and seismic platform for advocacy and sustainable equity. As the Founder and Executive Producer of the award-winning documentary, Beyond Their Years-The Incredible Legacies of Herb Carnegie and Buck O'Neil, for decades I have positioned the practice of Diversity, Equity, and Inclusion as essential elements to function as a leader. Tom Casey and* **Discussion Partner Collaborative** *have provided me with counsel and provocative research. I know Tom Casey to be an ally and this book on leadership will challenge, inform, and influence all of us.*

Wendy Lewis—Founder, AllySHIFT
Former McDonalds Global Chief Diversity Officer and
Head of Diversity for Major League Baseball

Tom Casey and I worked together at **The Concours Group** *a Research and Advisory firm. Over the last decade we have engaged in conversations regarding* *our aligned endeavors on leadership matters. With the dramatic shifts in the nature of work, impact of Generative AI, evolving workplace, climate, and globalization challenges future leaders must adopt substantially different mindsets and skills.* **Leadership's Future-Confronting Not Condoning!** *is a timely book given our current realities.*

Vaughn Merlyn—Principal The Merlyn Group LLC
Co-Founder and Fellow of The Business Relationship
Management Institute

I have worked with Tom Casey and **Discussion Partners** *in a variety of capacities for over 15 years.* **Leaderships Future-Confronting Not Condoning!** *is a must read for anyone interested in improving their organization through superior and effective leadership. When it comes to investing the most important trade you can make is avoiding the landmines. Tom and his collaborators do just that, as they expertly identify toxic traits leaders must avoid fostering healthy and productive environments. With real life examples and actionable advice the book highlights the pitfalls that can derail even the most well-intentioned leaders.*

Jay Pestrichelli—CEO & Co-Founder Zega Financial
LLC
Author of ***Buy & Hedge-The Top Five Rules for Investing Over the Long Term***

I was introduced to Tom Casey by his nephew David a highly decorated Educator and Coach. Since meeting we have been discussing the challenges facing women athletes, Title IX and the recent excitement of the NCAA Basketball event. Women athletes through their training and discipline are uniquely positioned post-graduate to endure bias. A consequence of their shared experience is a willingness to "create space" promoting an environment of compassion, active listening, and conviction in self worth. **Discussion Partners** *upcoming book,* **Leadership's Future-Confronting Not Condoning!** *Identifies Bias as a "reprehensible behavior." Women athletes can attest this is unacceptable and collaboratively we will challenge its existence.*

Dr. Kathleen Ralls—Founder KR LLC (Women's
Engagement & Empowerment)
Author of ***Take Her Word For It-Sports Cultivate World Class
Leaders*** and
***Voices of Title IX-Chelmsford High School Girl Athletes
and the Women They Became***

Tom Casey's invaluable advisory insights span three of the now four generations of our recently celebrated 100th anniversary of our family business. It's remarkable how he has maintained his relevancy, from his common military background with our WWII veteran Dad, to our Generation Z fourth generation. I believe his secret sauce of relevancy is a collective wisdom from constant old fashioned intense human interaction, across many industries, to his all in preparedness, supported by **Discussion Partner's** *research for blogs, articles, and books. I eagerly await strategizing with Tom to incorporate* **DPC's** *latest findings into our Succession and Leadership discussions.*

Michael Tomasso—Chairperson Board of Directors
Tomasso Group of Companies

Tom Casey and **Discussion Partners** *have done it again, only this time with a twist. Instead of researching and look at what effective leaders do, they looked at what they shouldn't do; a clever way to highlight what doesn't work. Ever experience someone who is inept but thought they were exceptional? Ever experience someone who thought they commanded a great team, only to see "group* *think" take over with everyone afraid to cross the boss? Well I have.* **DPC** *lays out a unique fact based perspective that we should use to gauge others and ourselves.*

Tom Wilson—Founder The Wilson Group
Author of *Next Stage: In Your Retirement Create The Life You Want* and the upcoming book *Concord's Wright Tavern: At The Crossroads of the American Revolution*

Dedications

To all the "Cs" in my life, US and Peruvian extended family. Shout out to my children Amy and Gordon and grandchildren Ada Zane, Thomas William, Zohy Dakota, and Alexander Upham: "I'm sorry my generation is leaving such a mess-Tda"

Tom

To my four grandchildren, Kinley, Evelina, Roman and Ledger. The world may look different once you exit high school, but the values identified in this book are timeless. Reach for the stars but never lose sight of who you are.

Claire

For my parents, Axel and Lauren Freudmann, who never give up. And my B Corp community who never stop striving. To everyone who has been too scared, too tired, or too busy to show up, but who showed up anyway. And to Dorit and Beth for your encouragement.

Elizabeth

To my brothers and sisters in arms, thank you for your guidance and showing me how to lead.

Sean

Table of Contents

Introduction

Picture a boss who the Analysts love for good reason but who has a leadership style reminiscent of Attila the Hun—whose egocentrism has them as "Me" in the Me Too movement in self-flattering terms and confuses DEI with Drug Enforcement.

Then ask yourself if you are working for this person, despite their success, does it connote respect?

The Chinese proverb "may you live in interesting times" according to Wikipedia is "ironic" as the word "interesting" connotes "times of trouble."

While one can quarrel, did the proverb originate with the Chinese; does "interesting" mean anything beyond its definition. Or is there an alternative assessment that will prompt conspiracy theories on social media?

The author's position is the proverb is applicable today, as we are in a time of trouble. The title-***Leadership's Future-Confronting Not Condoning!*** forcefully reminds all with the title "leader" their obligation to promote the interests of those being "led" relentlessly.

Unless one's domicile is on Mars, the inescapable reality is the onslaught of news promotes a premonition of impending chaos or for the eternal optimist unexpected surprises.

In 2021 **Discussion Partners Collaborative (DPC)** published *Leadership Development-The Next Curve to Flatten!*

Our research persuasively concluded that Associates have modified their demands of **all leadership cohorts** to embed *empathy, transparency, accountability,* and *collaboration* into necessary vs. preferred traits.

In early 2022 **DPC** embarked on a research study with one question:

"In rank order from 1-5, what are the most reprehensible leadership behaviors you are noting in our world"?

Utilizing pulse surveys, focus groups, and interviews with participants in our High Potential Development programs, we secured **1860** unduplicated responses (the rationale for suspending data collection at this number will be explained in a later chapter).

The "Top 5" identified as "reprehensible behaviors" in order are as follows:

1. **Hypocrisy**
2. **Bias**
3. **Intolerance**
4. **Expediency &**
5. **Aggressiveness**

In tandem to the collection of data, **DPC** began authoring a series of blogs disaggregating our research while linking back to these outcomes.

For this book, the authors have updated these blogs, augmenting with relevant topics, and aligned our narratives to these persuasive research findings.

Our objective utilizing this format is to make a case for **executive self-examination** posing the question:

Do you want your leadership legacy to be linked to any or worse all of these reprehensible behaviors?

Our "**Confronting Not Condoning**" reference connotes the need for leaders to ignore the surrounding chaos and earn their title via example, and if a reset is necessary, hesitation is not an option!

There may be a pre-disposition to associate reprehensible behaviors to the political arena, however the anecdotal feedback did not spare the commercial sector.

The top 3 areas of criticism of Commercial Leaders were as follows:

- **Immigration**—the confluence of no rational policy, over the top rhetoric, unresolved issue of "Dreamers" complicated by the chronic need for talented people-coalesced around the sentiment "the C-Suite should be doing more to pressure Congress vs. sitting on the side-lines"
- **Abandonment of DEI**—the lack of forceful support for; or worse diminished emphasis on this initiative, has not gone unnoticed
- **Women's Rights**—leaders not taking a stand on this matter is problematic as "hearing crickets at a time of crisis" is of concern to both genders

DPC did learn of a new metaphor "leaders are afraid to be Bud-Lighted."

The authors encourage you while reading this book to be mindful of a quote by Margaret Thatcher:

"Watch your thoughts because they become words. Watch your words because they become actions. Watch your actions because they become habits. Watch your habits because they become your character.

Tom Casey—Lincoln MA & Lima Peru
Claire Hebert-Dow—Laconia NH

Leadership's Future

Confronting Not Condoning!

Chapter 1
Discussion Partners Research Findings
2022-2024
(1860 Participants)

Leadership's Future-Confronting Not Condoning!

In late 2023 two articles were created to conduct a "looking forward in the rearview mirror." The objective was first to identify the concerns of our research participants as we entered 2024. In addition, presenting the abrupt shift in desired success behaviors derived from the Pandemic indicating "soft skills are necessary vs. 'nice to have'!"

- Controlling Epistemic Anxiety
- Leadership 2025 Remember to Breathe!

Controlling Epistemic Anxiety

Welcome to the New Year! 2024 portends to be a roller coaster ride geopolitically, economically, and socially.

Beginning late summer of 2023 in **Discussion Partners** research and client work we observed the manifestation of *"Epistemic Anxiety"* among those with whom we were interacting.

The clinical definition of epistemic anxiety is "a phenomenon that has been posited to undermine the motivation for stakes sensitive theories of knowledge." Translated into the sentiments being expressed to us were rage and lack of control resulting in a challenged optimism and concern for the future.

To dig deeper into the anecdotal feedback we had been receiving **DPC** conducted a Pulse Survey positing the following two questions:

1. As you envision 2024 what are the circumstances that give you cause for concern? And,
2. What societal influences migrate from concern to fear and/or rage?

There were 1213 respondents derived from our relationship base to the above two questions. Responses were persuasive leading **DPC** to conclude "folks are really fed up with the situation in the world overall, and leaders both political and commercial in particular."

Be advised this research effort coincided with the Hamas attack on Israel, concerns regarding the prosecution of the Israeli interdiction in Gaza, drama in respect to selection of a US Speaker of the House, 2024 anticipated global election concerns, debate as to need for, and appropriateness of, funding for Israel and the Ukraine war efforts concomitant to the US Immigration situation, and manifested concern for the projected vulnerability of Capital Markets.

For communication purposes **DPC** is organizing the responses to both questions into *"major causes for dissatisfaction and concern"* highlighting the top areas of consternation.

2024 Dissatisfaction Indices

- **Immigration**—this topic elicited the overwhelming sentiment that complaints about, posturing on, and denial of problem, are aggravating respondents' patience. Sentiments such as "shut up and fix the problem" were oft expressed. Political inertia was the most mentioned input. It was frequently noted that IF countries could come to grips with the challenge the chronic shortage of labor would be mitigated

- **Institutions**—the year over year decline of faith in **all** institutions (government, corporations, religious, media, and courts) was noted. Most frequently referred to in the US was the Supreme Court's decisions on Gun Control and Abortion as root causes for lack of faith (note the military in the US was positively commented upon by respondents)

- **Politics**—It is hard to know where to start on this one. Be advised we did ask respondents to self-identify their political spectrum position. Those who classified themselves as "Moderates" from both US parties and Internationally represented the overwhelming number of respondents. Candidly the lack of global progress to address serious issues such as Climate Change, Income Inequality, Immigration, as opposed to "self-serving posturing" were communicated as areas of friction. (There was unanimous agreement that the 2024 US Presidential elections will represent "referendum on democracy" observations also highlighted in December 2023 editions of *The Economist*, and *The Atlantic*)

- **Religion**—overt Anti-Semitism and intolerance of adherents to the Muslim faith globally were resoundingly criticized, exacerbated by the October 7th incursion into Israel and resultant human collateral casualty of the Gaza interdiction

- **Truth**—while the usual suspects Politicians and Media got the Pinocchio awards, no institution, faith, nor commercial sector was absent criticism. The most frequently mentioned example was the response to the Opioid Crisis and unwillingness to confront extremism as no-one's finest hour

- **Violence**—the violence visited upon of a "different race, religion, or sexual orientation" as evidenced by Illinois, Jacksonville, Charleston, Buffalo, Pittsburgh, SoCal killings domestically Ukraine, Sudan, Israel, and Gaza internationally. Three adjunct observations were ventured, 1. Promotion of White Supremacy, 2. Continued denial by the Courts, NRA, and Politicians that "the death of innocents will only increase until we deny access to assault weaponry" 3. The wars in Ukraine and Gaza concomitant with derived religious intolerance

- **Women**—while treatment, compensation parity, and career opportunity were mentioned the abandonment of Roe vs. Wade, and the attempts by certain countries (Poland), to oversee the choices women make on abortion among other matters were deemed as negatives (the political push back on these matters was celebrated as "victories" in Ohio, Kansas, and Poland)

- **War**—the War in the Ukraine as a test for NATO, Gaza, and tensions with Russia, and China contribute to a sense of malaise

Although not considered statistically significant as compared to above responses, concerns about AI, Elitism, Climate Threats and Economic Recession were identified. **McKinsey** *Insights* on December 12th reinforced these areas as C-Suite imperatives for 2024.

The overall conclusion from the **Discussion Partners** research is that concerns about the state of the world are influencing feelings of isolation, disenfranchisement, and in some cases personal depression.

When suggestions as to "how can your leaders help you navigate the upcoming year," **DPC** received input similar to our 2021 research as we emerged from the Pandemic. *Empathy*, *Transparency*, and *Accountability* were identified as not aspirations of leaders; they are now indicated as requirements.

In addition self-promotion, expediency, unwillingness to confront, and aspiration for media moments appear to be reaching their sell-by date of tolerance.

One quote encapsulated for **DPC** Advisors the overarching mental model as we enter the year, "During Covid we were terrified, subsequently there has been no real cause for optimism, compelling me to crave unselfish and constructive leadership on all levels."

Leadership 2025 Remember to Breathe!

In 1982, I (Tom) had been a consultant for a short time and attended the final briefing for regional bank reorganization. After agreement had been reached on structure, role architecture, etc., the client asked me, "OK, who should go in what box?"

Picture if you will the incredulous look of the bank's CEO and groans of my firm's senior Partners when my response was, "I don't know."

Afterwards, as was pointed out by the Partners at various decibel levels, the words "I don't know" should never pass the lips of a consultant in a client setting. My defense—reluctance to adjudicate an executive's career based upon a lack of agreed-upon criteria and 90 minutes of interaction—was unpersuasive.

Foreseeing my future as a Partner and sustainability as a Consultant likely truncated, out of desperation if not career survival, I developed a methodology whereby C-Suite-only executives were asked, "what are the differentiating skills that must be possessed by successful executives?"

Fast forward to the end of 2022—after 40 years, eight advisory firms and over 6,000 respondents, for the first time, my associates and I began seeing a lack of symmetry in respondent answers.

To put the above in context, our methodology groups findings into three separate areas.

1. *Threshold Attributes*—baseline proficiencies such as bias for action in solving problems respondents point out that if the executive avoids addressing, it becomes "theirs to resolve."

2. *Marketplace Positioning*—an example is industry/ sector trend prediction where the more successful executives can envision an opportunity while gathering necessary resources for exploitation in advance of competitors.

3. *Internal Influence*—the most prized skill within this segment is staff/subordinate development, the combination of a nose for talent with a reputation as a development sensei.

Since 1982, these methodology responses had been similar, if not exactly the same. Notwithstanding, for the better part of four decades, the adage "the more things change the more they remain the same" applied. The Pandemic and today's talent shortages have raised heretofore nice-to-have attributes to necessary-to-possess skills.

DPC research towards the end of the Pandemic was highlighted in our now-bestselling book **Leadership Development The Next Curve To Flatten!** Co-author Claire Hebert-Dow and I noted three leadership behaviors **empathy; transparency** and **accountability** are now must-haves for leaders to be perceived as "follower eligible."

Presently and in the future not having these traits in the managerial portfolio is at executive and enterprise expense. The following examples reinforce **DPC's** assessment methodology.

In April 2022, **Discussion Partners** posted a blog entitled *"Heads Up!"*—sharing our interactions with high potentials when the word "disgust" was used frequently.

As you might recall, at that time, the United States experienced several firsts: the slap seen around the world at the Oscars; the appointment of the first African American woman to the U.S. Supreme Court; and the gracelessness of only one Republican Senator standing in celebration of history and diversity.

Of course, these incidents were backlit by the real-time evidence of human tragedy in the Ukraine, now Israel, and Gaza.

As then stipulated, among the service offerings provided by **Discussion Partners** is *Next Gen Leadership Development*, where we focus on preparing future leaders for enterprise succession.

While discussing the input we were receiving, **DPC** internally began debating the question: Does America remains "exceptional" in our own eyes and in the eyes of our global neighbors?

The philosopher Tocqueville coined "American Exceptionalism" in 1831—the definition of the term is that the United States is "distinctive, unique or exemplary as compared to other nations."

DPC thought it would be useful to expand the base to encompass multiple generations and focusing on "Exceptionalism." This survey would examine the precipitous decline of faith in institutions as reported by various news outlets and research entities. For example, in September 2022, Gallup reported that trust in the Supreme Court had declined to 47%—a 20-year low! (June 2024 it is 39%) Congress, the Executive Branch and the Media did even worse.

Unfortunately, as we continue our national journey, **DPC** research concluded the level of irritation, distrust, impatience and disgust is by no means linked to "next gen" and is pan-generational.

DPC Pulse Survey (combined results Next Gen and Multi-Generational—982 respondents)

Survey question: Does the term American Exceptionalism still applies? (Please provide examples.)

Combined results:

- No—69%
- Yes—27%
- Don't Know—4%

Anecdotal Survey Comments

- *State of the Union*—heckling of President Biden-"Obama was called a liar once and we all recoiled. This time, it was perceived as normal." "I expected the Congresswoman to finish with the words 'pants on fire'!"

- *Mass shootings*—"We have more mass shootings than days in the year. Maybe we should expand the number of days to 730 and avoid embarrassment."

- *Speaker of the House dynamics*—"As if the selection process was not torture enough, during the State of the Union, we had to watch the then Speaker of the House, second in line for the Presidency, behave like an ignored daycare teacher uttering SSSSHHHHH to Caucus members."

- *Red state/Blue state "divorce"*—'We've already fought one Civil War because of succession." "Will I now need a passport to go home to Austin within Texas?"

- *Curriculum redesign and book removal*—"The step from anti-WOKE to Nazi-like suppression has been crossed." "Putin is laughing his ass off, good he has something to make him happy."

- *Toxic spill in Ohio*—"I would think the politicians would be more focused on how it happened and how to prevent it as opposed to posturing for the media."

- *Parental leave*—"The fact that this is not a core entitlement for United States citizens makes us look fourth world." "We are delusional when we say we promote family values." "Think about the pregnant women who are affected by this circus for Pete's sake."

- *January 6th debate*—"Get over it, folks. It happened, people died, and we look like idiots by denying it and not fixing the causes." "I sleep better now that the Panda protester has been arrested." (Reference to 2/27 arrest)

In previous blogs, podcasts and articles, **Discussion Partners** has asserted the following root causes for a lack of access to a robust talent pool and associate engagement:

- Shift in demographics—the consequence of disparity between and among birth, employment and death rates is the shortage of available workers.

- Life is too short—**DPC** has discerned those executives with means are curtailing their work life by either resigning now or consciously shortening their tenure, although the exodus has slowed as of late.

- Not 4 U, dudes!—There are more than a few workers who have decided, given the opportunities before them, that continuing to work in a situation where they feel undervalued and/or taken advantage of has an immediate sell-by-date! While the Great Resignation phase now has the Great Regret element, the difficulty in staffing remains a constant in many sectors.

- Lack of rational immigration policy—The challenges for talent readiness and inflation are negatively impacted by this political "third rail."

In our April 2022 effort, it was hard to quantify "disgust" as a trend. A year later, the expanded research sample unfortunately leads **DPC** to assert that the only Exceptionalism enjoyed the U.S. is we are becoming more polarized and intolerant of any opinion or constituency with which we don't identify.

In conclusion, while executive success factors like love are hard to quantify, the clear indication is that in 2020, expectations changed, and intolerance for leadership insincerity is now the rule.

Future leaders need to re-think their skillset to avoid the endangered species list.

Chapter 2

Hypocrisy
(1778 of 1860 Respondents)

No man for any considerable period can wear one face to himself and another to the multitude without finally getting bewildered as to which may be true.

—Nathaniel Hawthorne

#1 with a bullet! The participants using the political class as the primary, although not exclusive, offending constituency conveyed impatience with the assertion, "I would never" and then migrating to "of course I will." Such bravado can't mask the self-interest associated with a reversal of position.

Negative examples are too innumerable to mention and occur daily.

To avoid having to provide anti-depressants in conjunction with book sales, our positive examples focus on a politician while cognizant of risk promoted an initiative deemed important.

In addition, we offer a real-life demonstration of the value of collaboration where sublimation of ego works wonders.

- Consequences NOT The Priority
- Pilobolus 10 Years on Reminder of Lessons Learned

Consequences NOT the Priority

Winston Churchill stated, "To each there comes in their lifetime a special moment when they are figuratively offered a chance to do a very special thing!"

Speaker Johnson's allowing for a vote to be taken on Ukrainian aid represents this sentiment.

The definition of Motion Without Movement is "the technique for displaying patterns that appear to move continually without changing their positions."

While to some the United States Congress is the embodiment of this sentiment as institutions go, it is by no means alone. All sectors of society share the guilt of inactivity, insincerity, and inconsistency.

Unfortunately, the dysfunction is now the norm; and those who are well intentioned are at the mercy of the self-interested promoting their personal goals.

In researching our book *Leadership Development-The Next Curve to Flatten!* one's willingness to take risks independent of personal consequences were discerned as a necessary vs. nice-to-have leadership behavior.

To assess "public sector risk tolerance" in the waning months of 2023, **Discussion Partners** initiated a pulse survey asking our constituency: *"**If you were Speaker of the House Johnson, how would you handle the proposed aid package to Ukraine?**"*

DPC's intent was to assess the current reality of Motion Without Movement in tandem with the sentiments expressed in Churchill's quote.

Our objective was and remains the securing of data to better allow us to advise our C-suite and future leader clients in respect to their current circumstances.

Of the 428 respondents, over 80% were supportive of supplying aid. The anecdotal comments offered were candid in respect to positions on **NATO, Putin, Border, and Caucus Criticism.**

In tandem to the external survey, we asked those in our Partnership: *"Was there ever a political event that required leaders to take a position knowing he or she could become a casualty?"*

While there have been many examples (the McCarthy hearings, Civil & Voter rights referendums, and most recently Congresswoman Cheney's January 6 position), another event stood out to us—the Panama Canal Treaty of 1978 which was passed in the Senate by one vote!

At the time Majority Leader Harry Byrd was cognizant of the need to secure passage. He needed the support and advocacy of Minority Leader Senator Howard Baker.

Given the United States involvement in constructing the Canal, its critical role in respect to the global economy, and the political environment at the time when President Carter's popularity was waning, logic would dictate Senator Baker would distance himself from this initiative.

Senator Baker instead distinguished himself promoting the treaty and earning a later comment from Senator Byrd, "When I think of courage, I think of Howard Baker."

Speaker Johnson based upon our research most definitely exhibited courage, while ignoring the potential consequences, breaking the cycle of Motion Without Movement and exemplifying the Churchill quote.

At the risk of curing your insomnia by referencing additional research in 2021, Claire and I authored a blog on the findings we feel are material in today's leadership effectiveness environment.

The blog was entitled "Past Is Prologue" based upon Shakespeare's *The Tempest.*

The research derivative we maintain is appropriate today, encompassing the following suggestions to leaders as they ponder the consequences of controversial stands.

The ten anecdotal respondent quotes **DPC** *felt most insightful are as follows:*

- *In times of uncertainty before acting, be certain.*
- *Don't overreact to overreactions.*
- *Envision a future, work backwards, and embed alarms.*
- *Over communicate and then over communicate.*
- *Expand contrarian sources of information and synthesize input.*
- *Your Plan B should be as solid as Plan A.*
- *Surround yourself with folks who challenge your thinking vs. suck up to your position.*
- *Take stands that are risky-making statements of faith, values, and confidence.*

- *Don't be naïve about the risks of being right.*
- *Remember: 'Them R We.'*

As leaders, inertia, expediency, and conflict avoidance while normative, the willingness to exhibit courage is more widely respected.

To reinforce a point in the movie *Troy*, a young man stated to Achilles, "I would not fight this man. He is too big." Brad Pitt, in this role, uttered, "That is why no one will remember your name." Taking risks independent of consequences is memorable and respected—the opposite is a fast track to obscurity.

Pilobolus 10 Years on Reminder of Lessons Learned

As we complete the first quarter of 2024, the nature of collaboration as a forceful tenet of leadership remains elusive.

If you challenge this assumption, we need to relocate to wherever you reside. It would be great to turn off or reduce the noise level of the lack of cooperation and conflict for the sake of conflict that is emblematic of today's existence.

Ten years ago, Tom had the opportunity to attend an event of the dance ensemble Pilobolus, where the demonstration of collaborative behavior was extremely powerful resulting in a blog posted on various **DPC** platforms.

The lessons learned reinforced by attendance at the event, while still relevant, remain conspicuous by their absence in most ecosystems—particularly politics.

Two Discussion Partner research efforts in late 2023 highlighted the need bordering on craving for leaders, regardless of where they sit, to exhibit collaborative behaviors.

The first was a review of over 50 children's books where cooperation and teamwork were a universal thematic. The second was a survey of over 1200 executives who were highly critical of the absence of collaboration in pursuit of a higher purpose in our global political ecosystem.

Two events of the recent past promote the theorem that collaboration and mutuality of support are preferable to self-promotion and inertia.

The first was the collapse of a key roadway in the Greater Pennsylvania area on June 11, 2023. The event sourced "expert opinion" that it would be "months" before this key infrastructure would be repaired.

They were wrong, as the collaboration between and among responsible politicians, agency heads, and workers deploying a creative solution led to a resumption of traffic within 12 days!!!!!

The second happened on January 2 where in Tokyo a Japan Airlines A350 aircraft collided with a Coast Guard plane engulfing both in flames.

The mutual support and professionalism of the cabin crew led to the successful evacuation with no fatalities of 379 "souls" within minutes!

In the political domain, partisanship above all else is the rule. A quote from Juan-Claude Juncker, former President of the European Commission, is illustrative: "Politicians know what is the right thing to do. What they don't know is how to get re-elected if they do."

The most recent examples in the US were the tanking of the bi-partisan Immigration Bill created in the Senate, loss of the Speakership of Kevin McCarthy for the temerity of involving Democrats in support of avoiding a government shutdown. Both incidents continue to have derivative real and implied threats associated with bi-partisan collaboration leading to policy paralysis.

Self-absorption and selfishness are alive and well in ALL sectors at the expense of the greater good on micro and global levels.

As we navigate what will be a critical year, collaboration should be a personal and collective objective as defining behaviors of "for me to win, someone has to lose" is self-defeating, observable, and based upon **DPC** research has the consequence of mitigation if not elimination of trust.

Picture the calamity of a Pilobolus event if the definition of success was individual vs. collective. Disastrous results would be guaranteed.

Original Post April 2014

The term Pilobolus refers to a fungus whose spores propel with extraordinary speed, accuracy, and strength. It is also a creative dance company founded by Dartmouth College students in the 1970s!

The dance company has survived and prospered on a global scale for 50 years incorporating innovation, education, and creativity!

My wife and I attend many dance company presentations from ballet through modern platforms. Yet the recent performance of this troupe in Boston was unlike any we have ever seen.

The degree of collaborative precision and feats of strength were magnificent to behold.

The six dancers are incredibly strong and flexible. Your emotions range from envious wondering how come you're three times a month visit to the gym for 30 minutes does not have a similar outcome. In addition, but certainly not least, you sit in wonder questioning whether or not their skeletal frameworks are calcium or silly putty based.

Unusual for us, we decided to stay to participate in the cast post performance Q&A.

The conclusion we drew, and the derived lessons learned for commercial enterprises were threefold.

- Each member of the company was encouraged to contribute to the choreography process regardless of tenure or role. It is not a "leader led only" organization.
- Each member of the company felt a degree of ownership due to this approach, therefore raising their already high level of accountability for and proficiency in the performance.
- The mutuality of respect and encouragement raises the level of creative input, excitement and innovation.

This feedback from the Company was unambiguous in respect to the above creating a "community" or "family" feeling.

How they approach their craft has many lessons learned for commercial enterprise leaders! The scary truths based upon **Discussion Partners** advisory experience is for the most part global leaders are slow learners as it relates to collaboration.

The five principles that **DPC** reinforces when speaking or facilitating on the topic of collaboration were present in abundance during the experience:

1. Clarity Regarding Roles
2. Exhaustive Preparation
3. Mutual Trust
4. Creative Input Encouraged Regardless of Tenure
5. Shared Mindset for Success Delineation

What the experience also underscored is that in collaborative processes, EGO IS THE ENEMY!!

If not, why are we so challenged in the commercial sector to achieve collaboration beyond lip service and generous self-serving interpretations of the word?

What was most compelling in the Pilobolus experience is for collaboration to be achieved, their shared mindset was: egos must be minimized; engagement maximized; respect optimized; and mutual trust epitomized.

Among many of life's mysteries, one that hopefully we can resolve soon, and Pilobolus has, is how to translate the abstract thinking as to how collaboration can be achieved moving it to reality from aspiration.

Chapter 3
Bias
(1689 of 1860 Respondents)

What a sad era when it is easier to smash an
atom than a prejudice

—Albert Einstein

The designation of #2 in the feedback connotes the increased awareness that one is encouraged not to believe what they see, hear, or take the time to secure any data to support decisions.

Bias has been a constant since the Garden of Eden and to pretend otherwise is ignoring the facts that surround us. Charlottesville, murder of George Floyd, anti-Semitism and Muslim respect derived from the Hamas attack on 10/07/23, LBGTQ rejection, and gender discrimination is overt and far-reaching.

A quote from a research participant "bias is now a badge of honor" is illustrative. The overarching sentiment of participants is that bias, when exhibited by an ostensible leader, is diminishing.

A form of bias as demographics shift is Ageism. David Bowie once asserted, "Aging is an extraordinary process where you become the person you always should have been."

As getting older is a common human condition and as one age's you are perceived differently, and due to this *bias* your capabilities questioned, these two articles should provide perspective.

- **Relevance-Who Did You Used to Be?**
- **No Is a Complete Sentence!**

Relevance—Who Did You Used to Be?

In 1995 during an expatriate assignment in Latin America, Tom found himself one weekend in Mexico City. He had worked with a client all day forgoing any food and went in search of an early dinner.

In pursuit of some sustenance, he passed by a restaurant whose band was playing soft rock music while serving its customers. The group was quite good, so he took a seat and ordered a meal along with a Pacifico beer. As the service was slow, he was on his second beer when the food arrived. It was inedible and he now thought it best to leave and pursue room service at his hotel.

The adjustment to the Mexico City altitude in conjunction with alcohol slogging on an empty stomach was catching up with him.

As he waited for the bill, the band returned and asked if anyone wanted to sing with them.

In his misspent youth Tom was a musician and his appreciation of the cohesiveness of the band was what drew him into the restaurant in the first place.

In his now addled brain, these disparate thoughts came together:

1. No one knows me
2. My resistance Is down (feeling no pain)
3. It has been ages since I sang

The confluence of the above led Tom to conclude 'Oh what can go wrong' inviting himself onto the stage.

The band seeing this older gringo dressed in jeans, cowboy boots, and bomber jacket and as usual in need of a haircut was taken by surprise. When asked, "What do you want to sing?" Tom stated, "After the Gold Rush, I'll sing you folks join in."

He got through the song and the applause, more likely due to politeness, was quite positive.

As he was leaving the stage, the bandleader asked, "Another one?" Now ego had inserted itself, "Sure. I'll sing *Danny Boy*." Given an Irish ballad was not in their song list, he just sang it a cappella.

Somewhere during the bridge of the song, his circumstances overtook his bravado, and he felt a sense of urgency to finish while thinking: "What in the hell am I doing up here?"

As he left the stage a young woman approached asking the question, "Who did you used to be?"

Unfortunately, for many executives this is the concern they are navigating as they transition. The fear is their next stage positions life in the "past tense," and they will no longer be *Relevant!*

No successful executive is absent a healthy degree of self-confidence and has kept score via promotions, title, and compensation. Leaving the "stage," regardless of age or reason, raises feelings of forsaken identity.

In **Discussion Partners** experience working with over 900 transitioning executives, we have found the preoccupation that "I am no longer relevant" to be the biggest what we refer to as the "contentment challenge."

In our experience reality is quite different! As Tammy Erickson, Ken Dychtwald and Bob Morison presented in their book *Workforce Crisis* and subsequent writings, assert careers are a series of "on ramps and off ramps."

Dr.'s Lynda Gratton and Andrew Scotts books on the topic particularly *The 100 Year Life* reinforces the concept of looking forward vs. over one's shoulder. Dr. Andrew Scott's book on Longevity reinforces this premise as well.

Tom recently attended a session at the **Modern Elder Academy,** in Baja Mexico co-founded by Chip Conley a prolific author on the topic of ageing in his recent book *Learning To Love Midlife* where he espoused the same message.

The consolidation of the above authors scholarship and experience design, when coupled with **DPC's** client involvement reinforce an alternative view: ***"Relevance is how you channel your energies, derive satisfaction, and self-assess outcomes."***

As we enter the end of year, it is a time when executives reflect on, "What's next?" In the strongest possible terms, **DPC** would recommend you not be anxious your relevance is suspended if you transition. It is more likely you will find an alternative lane for expression.

In closing **DPC** recommends the military premise of looking "over the horizon" disregarding concerns of relevance as you envision your next stage.

"No" Is a Complete Sentence!

Tom had the great fortune in March to attend a weeklong event at the Modern Elder Academy in Baja Mexico. MEA is the brainchild of Chip Conley whose books on Transitions and Rejuvenation are standards for those whose commercial focus is on this topic and for the over 3000 folks who have attended their workshops. Chip's newest book entitled *Learning To Love Midlife: 12 Reasons Why Life Gets Better With Age* was released in January 2024.

He arrived exhausted after having worked in South America and the US Northeast and very cynical as to whether this sojourn was a constructive use of his time.

Upon returning without hesitation stipulated that once he disengaged from his self-absorption, he benefitted from the **MEA** experience. Most importantly was the creation of a new network of folks whom he would otherwise never have met.

Among the participants was a California based Attorney Jack Russo, host of the Podcast *The Valley Current* whom strongly recommended the book *Essentialism* by Greg McKeown.

During his post-event travels he read the book and came across the quote by Anne Lamott an accomplished non-fiction writer whose scholarship is often referred to for guidance.

The quote that resonated forcefully was, *"No Is A Complete Sentence"*!

In **Discussion Partners** work with High Potentials we have discerned an intensifying level of dissatisfaction bordering on militancy beginning in 2020 among those deemed "ready now" and "investment worthy" in Succession plans.

Since April 2020 in our blogs, podcasts, and book *Leadership Development-The Next Curve To Flatten!* we have been deploying the services of our now totally exhausted Survey Monkey, attempting to secure fact-based insights as to where trust in leadership took such a dramatic detour.

DPC's research findings have been unanimous for three years in that these cohorts expect in leaders **empathy, transparency, and accountability.** This hypothesis has been supported by other entities pondering the same question.

Gallup, McKinsey *Insights, Financial Times,* and *Wall Street Journal* as well as virtually every media outlet have commented on the disenfranchisement of the "Next Generation of Leaders."

The consensus has been that this constituency's relocations to alternative employment settings (The Great Resignation, Migration, Re-Negotiation) have been driven by the plethora of post-Pandemic opportunities.

Discussions Partners ongoing research on "root causes" strongly suggest that the motivation for employer change and/or irritation with the "state of the world" is not as easily explained.

In the recent past issues such as the Nashville School shooting resulting in the deaths of 2 9-year old children, followed by the expulsion of two legislators of color who had manifested their right to free speech, and clearly having a moral compass chose to protest, the Texas Judges reversal of over 20 years of medicinal access by women allowing for their right to choose, the war in the Ukraine, and the awareness that as of April while there were 121 days in the year there had been 184 Mass Shootings (**MSNBC)** do not inspire confidence that leaders "get it."

Moreover what is becoming abundantly clear is that employers should not be lulled into a false sense of optimism the layoffs of the recent past will mitigate the difficulties in finding and retaining new talent.

Using the recent numbers in the US for example there are still approximately 1.5 available jobs for each searching worker despite the month over month increase of folks returning to the workforce.

The confluence of the above and our April 2023 study of over 500 Millennials lead **DPC** to the conclusion that Ms. Lamott's quote of "No is a complete sentence" is applicable. Absent enterprises and leaders manifesting an awareness of, and willingness to, be advocates for overt change, when offered opportunities they will state **"NO"**!

Chapter 4

Intolerance

(1668 of 1860 Respondents)

Intolerance is of itself a form of violence and an obstacle to the growth of a true democratic spirit.

—Mahatma Gandhi

It is hard to capture the participant emotion associated with the #3 example of reprehensible behavior. It is analogous to a conversation one would want to have with an ex-spouse where the refrain ". . . and another thing" is oft repeated.

The concepts of White nationalism, Christian nationalism, rejection of the aspirations of immigrants, and anti-LBGTQ rhetoric are a constant.

A representative quote from an Medical Doctor, LBGTQ immigrant to Canada from South Korea provides an interesting vantage point: "I wanted to be in a country where I didn't have to say shut your mouth and open your mind."

The two writings are a celebrity example of an individual who demonstrated unequivocal courage. The second is a more historical analysis of intolerance.

- *Intolerance-A Turning Point Not Taken!*

- *In Praise of Caitlyn (Competitively Known as Bruce) Jenner*

Intolerance-A Turning Point Not Taken!

The British historian AJP Taylor once used the term "The turning point not taken" to describe decision-making inertia. This reference is representative of intolerance that is accelerating in many global societies. The consequence of today's reality is this intolerance is disenfranchising companies.

In the recent past in the United States, we have experienced the undeclared war between Governor DeSantis of Florida and Mickey Mouse while suggesting Slavery was a career skill enhancer.

Also, we are aware of the boycotts of Chick-fil-A driven by their position of not deploying political criteria in advance of ordering a sandwich despite their faith-based business model.

In the context of irony, Bud Light due to its use of LGBTQ "Influencer" has been boycotted to the point they lost their #1 market share to Modelo, which is essentially a Mexican beer. Good thing for supply chain issues the "Wall" remains an abstract idea.

Issues such as political polarization, gun control, women's right to choose, and extremism tolerance all are now day-to-day societal challenges.

In addition, it's apparent our political landscape is continuing its anti-immigration posture despite self-evident economic implications. This is despite the chronic labor shortage and the predictions by advisors such as **Goldman Sachs** that the lack of a "rational immigration policy fuels inflation" (May 2022).

In the context of racism, we had the Charleston shooting and Charlottesville white supremacist march with reactions aggravating the racial tensions in the United States. Any citizen who is unaware that the white supremacist is not finding an audience is not paying attention. The shootings in El Paso and Buffalo now receive a shrugged shoulder "another one."

Police reactions to racial relations are strained and satirized by comedians venturing: "The only ways to avoid being shot are: a) don't wear a hoodie; b) don't be big . . . and c) don't be black." Somehow, we think this is funny!

The murder of George Floyd and the global rejection of this type of behavior as excusable assaulted our consciousness, proving that institutional racism is a fact of our existence that should be confronted.

It is easy to be cynical when we hear the words "Black lives matter" and respond with "All lives matter." Yet our reality is much different. The progress of the #Me Too Movement does not appear to have made much of a difference in racial relations. The challenges to "WOKE" are non-sensical on any logical level as is the rejection of the advocacy of Diversity Equity and Inclusion (DEI).

We are all intolerant to a degree. This trait is not part of our DNA but a learned behavior. The question before any individual believing himself or herself to be racially, politically, socially tolerant is twofold: a) how do you know if your self-image of tolerance is delusional; and b) what do you do if faced with your subconscious intolerance?

Independent of our self-image for openness, political mindset, and understanding of the evolution of racial relations in the United States, based upon a recent **Discussion Partner** research one conclusion is unassailable: *ignoring institutional intolerance is commercially self-destructive.* If an organization or political entity has a reputation of intolerance, it disenfranchises their brand reputation and economic viability.

Years ago, as preparation for our book *Executive Advice To The Young-Don't Repeat My Mistakes!*, **DPC** was fortunate to find an executive who was willing to share his experiences. What is of particular interest is this executive previously held Congressional office and was known as an advocate for tolerance on all levels.

Executive Interview Former Congressman

During my formative years I was privileged. Consequently, my personal philosophy and points of view about race relations, immigration and other issues were based on reading and discussions, not experience.

I always thought of myself as tolerant regarding people who were different whether it was race, political orientation, sexual preference, etc.

Unfortunately, I was wrong....

I was giving a speech out of state and got lost on the way back to the airport.

This was in the days before I-phones. Lost meant lost. I had an associate with me who was driving the rental car.

We wandered into a distressed neighborhood and stopped to get our bearings. I noticed three young men of color not far away who were clearly aware of our presence. We were unsettled. They started walking toward us and in an attempt to drive away, crashed the car.

They kept coming . . . now running. When they got to us, they said: "Are you guys ok?" "Do you need some help?" They could not have been nicer. They got us to the airport, arranged for a rental car company. They were great.

Flying back home, I could not help thinking about how scared I was and why. Clearly it was the neighborhood, the circumstances and more importantly, the three young men being Black.

I asked myself this question: Even in a rough neighborhood, if they were White, dressed in khakis wearing IZod shirts, would I have reacted the same way?

Clearly not . . .

What also got my attention was when I relayed what happened to others. Their response was disheartening as they commented: "I would have been scared too." Also, "you got lucky."

When I look back on that event, I realized that even with a narrow definition of the word, I am a racist. It shook my self-image and now I try to be mindful of 'who I am, not who I thought I was'.

The question before me at that time and now is to channel this awareness, minimizing the damage it can cause and maybe even using the awareness to do some good.

Business Case 2024 Realities

The openness of the official was refreshing. His candor allows for the derivation of forceful questions:

- We are all intolerant of some things or many things, but how do we address challenges to our self-image when confronted?

- When we are confronted with our true beliefs or tendencies, we can behave in one of two ways: Ignore it or attempt to channel it in appropriate ways?

Self-awareness is an asset; self-respect an aspiration; self-direction, an obligation when our bias is inappropriate.

For business leaders there is a mental model that is emerging based upon **DPC** research: "conservative on economics; moderate on social causes." The post-Pandemic leadership nexus compels empathy, transparency, and accountability as "must haves" for leaders to be followed and their enterprises successful.

Absent an acknowledgement that institutional intolerance exists, and candidly is being encouraged, for commercial leaders a willingness to confront is an enterprise imperative: "If not now, when?"

As we envision 2025, it is advisable to do a reset on many topics among which is to "avoid avoiding" institutional bias as a problem that is not only societal, but just "bad business practice."

*In Praise of Caitlyn (Known Competitively as Bruce) Jenner—
Recognition of Courage & Tolerance*

1976 was a seminal year for the United States as we celebrated our bicentennial and admired an Olympic hero, then known to the world as Bruce Jenner.

Jenner won the Decathlon—a feat that to this day inspires envy among those of us who feel that "roughing it" is when we are in search of batteries for a failing remote control.

As is the wont of Olympic superstars, after gracing the cover of a Wheaties box, they'll try acting, being a pitch person, game show participant—even a host on SNL.

Jenner's courage and transparency were on display once again when Jenner "came out" as transgender on national TV in September 2015 announcing a name change to Caitlyn.

I would be hard pressed to find anyone who does not recognize the degree of discipline necessary to win an Olympic event and the risk of ridicule (among other dangers) for announcing this newest journey nearly a decade ago.

In February I attended the opening of *"Becoming a Man"* at the Harvard Theater in Boston. The play was written by a trans man and was an outstanding portrayal of the new complexities in the lives of those who take the step to publicly affirm their gender.

At least as helpful as the play, to me—an older Boomer man who acknowledges discomfort with those who have chosen same sex relationships—was the after-play discourse. Audience members who identified with the transgender experience shared their stories.

I came away in awe of their courage and willingness to pursue their journey independent of what others may think of their decisions.

In today's environment the behaviors of intolerance, expediency and self-absorption are widely accepted, if not celebrated.

Systemic racism, anti-Semitism and Islamic intolerance are normative, if not endorsed perspectives. This manifests as condoned violence.

In today's political ecosystem, the courage of a Liz Cheney or an Adam Kinzenger to challenge the rhetoric that diminishes the Constitution knowing full well it disenfranchises their political career is unusual.

As we navigate our times, in DPC's work with High Potentials and C-Suite Executives the words "character is more important than brains" represents the overarching sentiment concomitant to the disdain for leaders who exhibit hypocritical behavior.

As humans we admire courage and discipline whether it be in sports, politics, military service, or found in other arenas.

All of us know folks who are living examples of courage and who, despite risk, do the right thing because it is the right thing.

Unfortunately, we also know or are aware of those who have chosen self-interest.

In our unguarded moments we **all** embrace and respect courage wondering, if challenged, how we would act. Moreover, there is a dilemma of tolerance initiated when someone whose courage we admire espouses views we do not embrace.

As the 2024 Olympics approach I have begun thinking of Jenner and those in the audience of *"Becoming a Man"* as role models for courage, while in the case of Jenner, disagreeing with her political views.

As an advisor to C-Suite executives I am constantly looking for examples of fact- based decisions and recognizable examples of courage, while exercising tolerance when disagreeing with decisions and views.

Tolerance is to be expected, intolerance rejected; and for those who don't respect differences, it is doubtful you will ever win a Gold medal, or even more meaningful, be respected by peers and associates.

Chapter 5
Expediency
(1641 of 1860 Respondents)

Cowardice asks the question is it safe? Expediency asks the question is it politic?

—Dr. Martin Luther King Jr.

The term drinking from a fire hose came to mind as we reviewed the examples of expediency, none of them flattering.

The visibility and lack of apology resulted in its position as #4 designation for reprehensible behavior. The examples of narcissism, greed, unwillingness to confront, self-promotion, and stunted compassion constituted an interesting read.

Immigration is a global challenge. In 2015 we saw the body of a child who drowned in Europe. In the States we saw and see families broken up, razor wire, threats of detention camps, and posturing politicians dressed up like Border Control agents.

In 2023 expediency hit a new high or low depending on how one keeps score when a former President blunted a bi-partisan effort for political reasons. The plain sight effort sent his party scurrying for rationales, reminiscent of trying to explain why the earth is flat.

In June 2024 we saw this same cohort bemoan President Biden's Executive Order on Immigration many of the tenants contained in the bi-partisan effort as a "political ploy"

As a reminder to leaders how the next generation perceives expediency we are sharing an Op-Ed by Elizabeth Freudmann on the complexity of the journey for Millennials.

As you peruse these blogs think on Logan Roy in the series *Succession* when he stated to his children, "you are not serious people."

- ***Immigration-The Need For Solutions Not Rhetoric!***

- ***Unprecedented Times Require Integrity and Realism*** **(Elizabeth Freudmann)**

Immigration-The Need For Solutions Not Rhetoric!

The January 2017 Executive Order issued by the Trump administration banning entrant from select Muslim countries, had significant repercussions none of them good from a global policy or optics perspective.

The June 21st 2018 cover of *Time* magazine depicting a crying migrant child at the feet of the former President derived from the decision to separate families made a powerful statement about the culture of the US.

Two truths can exist at the same time 1. The lack of a rational immigration policy for the US despite years of debate is a failure of our political eco-system, and 2. Most of the 300M human beings who populate the US are the progeny of immigrants.

The consequence of former President Trump and Stephen Millers Immigration policies disguised as jingoism have diffused energy while polarizing the body politic in the US. Although in fairness the problem is systemic, suffering from benign neglect for quite some time.

In December of 2023 **Discussion Partners** published a Research Study where over 1000 respondents labeled our societies lack of a comprehensive Immigration policy as an "embarrassment," and "failure" referenced the decades long debate as "reprehensible."

As we end Q-1 of 2024 the discourse has devolved even further introducing words like "vermin", "detention camps" and "dumping the illegals in sanctuary cities" into the narrative.

A derivative of **DPC's** research is that respondents are enraged at the "self promotion", "expediency", "polarizing language" and "deliberate obtuseness" being deployed by our elected representatives vs. co-creation of a realistic solution.

As third generation immigrants, Claire and I thought it useful to re-share this chapter from **DPC's** book *Executive Advice To The Young-Don't Repeat My Mistakes!*

While this chapter references the aftershocks of 9/11 it is illustrative in that dramatic events evoke challenges personally and politically.

All of us could benefit from a reminder that it is important to live and act on our values, as being Patriotic is insincere without being Principled.

The Economist, The Atlantic, in December 2023, and the January publication of "Top Risks" by **The Eurasia Group** promote a perspective that our democracy is made up of politicians who are always at a crossroads, they can avoid expediency or concede to self interest.

As it relates to Immigration the electorate is finding the lack of bipartisan workable solutions overdue as summarized in a quote from the **DPC** study "they are all clowns in the same circus which I hope leaves town soon."

Original Posting May 2016

As part of an upcoming book on *Executives Advice to Children* based upon difficult experiences Tom interviewed a Boston based gentleman whom had an extensive career in the US military as a senior reserve officer in tandem with his commercial role.

The executive was commenting on the post-Paris terror reactions in the US where candidates were debating the wisdom of registration by religious affiliation . . . a position that he found "embarrassing as an American and moreover a human being." Below is the interview.

September 11th changed much for us in the States. We no longer felt safe, and for the most part unclear who was the enemy as in decades past it was a country vs. a country not a society vs. a religious belief kidnapped by extremists for their own purposes.

I have to say though that in the aftermath I behaved very badly on one specific occasion for which I am still ashamed.

About a week after 9/11 I boarded a plane from Boston to Dallas. I was upgraded to First Class, as the plane was somewhat empty.

Shortly after I boarded another passenger came on who looked of Arabic descent. I gave him a look that at best could be described as rage if not overtly threatening.

Immediately after he took his seat, also in First Class I took off my belt, rolled it up into a garrote, and covered it with my jacket. Candidly I don't know what I would have done if he had moved towards the cockpit . . . likely something stupid.

Fortunately, he did not get out of his seat. When we landed, I felt awful and guilty.

I waited for him in the terminal and apologized for the look I gave him with the words. I am sorry, that was inappropriate, and I thought I was better then that.

The man was startled that I took the time, he was Iranian and had come to the States as a student in the 80s and never went back due to the change in leadership and society culture.

He did say I guess I have to get used to people being suspicious and focusing their anger on me-I am angry too for what has been done to us!

In when considering our 2024 position when asked for his thoughts on the above he stipulated:

- I remember most he used the word us! This man felt the same way I did about the terrorist attack.

- It is dangerous to blame a society, religion, or philosophy for the actions of a few who interpret by self indulgence

- Other than Native Americans all in the US have immigrant origins ... the only question is how many generations between our ancestors and us ... ignoring this or forgetting is self serving at best

Politicians "fact finding" by visiting the borders, bussing exhausted humans to alternative locations to reinforce a political position, building walls, or blaming the "other party," won't solve addressing this problem.

As we are in the political season, we should ask incumbents and candidates the question, "what are you prepared to do, even if it is at your own expense"?

Unprecedented Times Require Integrity and Realism (Elizabeth Freudmann Op Ed)

Have you heard that old idiom that goes "if you're conservative when you're young, you have no heart; if you're liberal when you're old, you have no brain?" Perhaps you're familiar with its more capitalistic cousin that suggests that if you're liberal when you're old, "you have no money."

Are these hackneyed phrases distinctly American? Maybe they have parallel versions in other cultures or languages, but growing up in the United States, they seeped into my consciousness when I was still a child. Even then, the sentiment has consistently struck me as cynical, self-serving, and permissive. I've always had the sense that it is used as a sort of immunization against confronting our own selfishness as we mature. Instead of asking ourselves "what changed?" we can instead say "this is natural and therefore, right."

Now, as an older Millennial, neither the supposed reckless idealism of youth nor the self-interested survivalism of age feels appropriate to me, which it turns out, is a good thing. In 2024, neither attitude is practical. We have lived through too many unprecedented times to believe that old norms are still applicable (if they ever were). As far as having brains or money, if you have the former, it's hard to pretend that everyone has the same chance to amass the latter.[1] The public has too much information on generational wealth and income inequality to fall for that. Besides, what do the words "liberal" and "conservative" mean anymore? Those who declare themselves the arbiters of such things have set the bar of "belonging" so high that aspirants must be nothing short of zealots, unflinchingly dogmatic at all times. Practicality be damned!

The black-and-white thinking required to strive for belonging in either narrowly defined camp is unrealistic for those of us living in the real world. Down here, things are too complicated to fit into tidy boxes: maybe we *want* to believe it when our faith declares same-sex partnerships to be morally wrong, but we just can't bring ourselves to condemn our gay child. Or, some Americans might appreciate the horror of our frequent school shootings and find themselves thinking that while the right to bear arms is sacred, it's *also* just too easy for sick people with bad intentions to get their hands on dangerous guns. We can strive for a more equitable and just world *while* knowing that sometimes we're just going to get it wrong—as individuals, as communities, as countries, as a species.

But that doesn't absolve us from trying. And wow, do we need to try! The moral purists leading the culture wars appear to be more

---

[1] Lewis, C. (2024, February 10). Wealth disparities by race grew during the Pandemic, despite income gains, report shows | AP News. AP News. https://apnews.com/article/racial-wealth-inequality-Pandemic-stocks-pensions-f9b2eace6cd89807e5331f613f270da1

interested in winning rhetorical points on social media than in actually resolving anything. Meanwhile, wars rage, infrastructure collapses, healthcare systems around the world continue to fail, and the existential threat of the climate crisis looms large, begging the question: what are we leaving for Gen Alpha[2] and their children? Do we really want to do as that old idiom would suggest and leave the hard work of advocacy and social change to the young?

I would argue that no, we definitely do not want to do that. Not if we want to ensure that there's a habitable planet for our children and grandchildren. Youthful idealism is good as far as it goes, but experience, connections, perspective, and resources are required to turn all those good intentions into meaningful impact. And who has those? The elders of course, those who conventional wisdom would have us believe are (or should be) letting their metaphorical hearts harden as they lean conservative in order to husband their resources and protect their peace.

Personally, I don't know too many Boomers with hardened hearts, which is good because as of August, 2023, they still control more than half the wealth in the United States.[3] Nevertheless, despite their resources, many Boomers I know and love have opted to remain in the workforce well into their 70s—even when they have the means to retire. They are not alone: heading into the 2024 United States Presidential Election, it's painfully obvious that Boomers still control the levers of society that impact us all.

Boomers, you have opted to forgo the dream of spending your golden years relaxing with friends and family. I know you're still

[2] Eldridge, S. (2024, March 29). Generation Alpha. Encyclopedia Britannica. https://www.britannica.com/topic/Generation-Alpha

[3] Mae, A. (2023, August 27). More than half of US wealth belongs to baby boomers: Will other generations catch up? Nasdaq. https://www.nasdaq.com/articles/more-than-half-of-us-wealth-belongs-to-baby-boomers:-will-other-generations-catch-up

showing up to work (remotely or in person) 3-5 days a week. Who are you showing up for? Why them? You have resources, most especially wisdom, that the rest of us need, and there's only so long we can keep the dream of the future alive when we are being devoured—and exhausted—by the urgency of the present. Not to sound dramatic but if you care about what's next for humanity, now is the time to step up.

Now is also the time for all of us to let go of the obsession with labels and identity, and the policing of group belonging that have dominated the discourse for so long. Those rules do not apply anymore because there are too many and they are too exacting to be useful. We have to find a way to build coalitions that bridge generations, job titles, and demographics. We have to work collectively to develop actual solutions and spend less time on rhetorical social media wars. We can't keep leaving the hard work to the next generation. It's time to collaborate and get creative—to stop looking to the same people, the same systems, and the same solutions that haven't worked in the past.

Over the last few years I've heard more and more people share several versions of a new truism that feels much more appropriate for our current world: "nobody is coming to save us." "It's up to us to figure it out." "Start where you are, use what you have, do what you can." It is definitely more than a little scary to realize how completely the systems we trusted have failed us, and that the world depends on all of us wanting and trying to figure out a better way. But that's also exciting and liberating, don't you think? I've been trying and I will keep trying, the best way I know how. I hope you'll join me, because I truly believe that "only all of us can save us now."

Chapter 6

Aggressiveness
(1601 of 1860 Respondents)

Our hope should become that aggression is recognized as the sin that it is.

—Secretary of Defense General Lloyd Austin (Retired)

D-Day Remarks, January 6, 2024

#5 is exemplified by honking horns, rude language, obscene gestures, lack of social media restraint, and when arriving at the Punchbowl or campaign event name calling, insulting, ridiculing, and offering theories not substantiated by facts, some politico's typical day!

Although not limited to this cohort, the sentiments conveyed in **DPC's** research focused primarily on the lack of decorum exhibited by the political sector.

While not localized to the US nor Politicians, the decline in respect, and obliteration of partisanship since 2015 is the most frequently mentioned example of aggressiveness unchecked.

Bully's identify and encourage their admirers and via intimidation enjoy influence. They are rarely respected, and when no longer feared, fade to a footnote.

The article below we trust is illustrative.

Billy Got Big!

Welcome to Spring! The weather appears to be contributing to an uplifting of spirits. This is a non-trivial achievement given the inexhaustible sources of news suggesting if not worried about democracy, climate change, air travel, inflation, and warfare, you should start considering alien invasions.

If the recent past has taught us nothing, it is the undeniable fact that bullying behavior is now an overt core element of our existence. Invasions of neighboring countries, social media lack of restraint, ridicule of political opponents, intolerance of religion, violence associated with political issues, and polarizing language have become so pervasive, we are now numb.

In 2016 **Discussion Partners** published *Executive Advice To The Young-Don't Repeat My Mistakes,* various associations and distribution channels adjudicated the book a "best seller."

The book was targeted for a readership of 11- to 18-year-olds. The impetus was **DPC's** then collective frustration and candidly rage with the condition of the world and the negative role models we adults manifested for our children and grandchildren.

The book focused on issues such is diversity, honesty, respect, and bullying among others. The intent via interviews with executives was to recount a negative event, share outcomes and reinforce through storytelling their continued personal embarrassment years later.

Our intent was to suggest when children are faced with choices . . . it is best to make the appropriate ones to prevent or at least forestall damage to themselves or others.

Given our 2024 current reality bullying is alive and well . . . unfortunately promoted by social media and political discourse, leading to devastating results. Politics where explosive words, disrespectful behaviors, supported by audience laughing are the most frequently mentioned arenas for bullying by our clients.

Every study that discusses suicide in the younger generation references social media if not a root cause, infers its contribution. A recent study concluded that due to social media approximately 14% of the teenage population has contemplated suicide or self-harm.

This is wrong on many levels and if we as citizens have devolved to this level of pettiness, God help us!

Consequently the re-sharing of a Chapter from our book as a not so gentle reminder that bullying may be inadvisable for what should be self-evident reasons.

As you peruse the below . . . be mindful that the fervent hope of the **DPC** Partners is if you initiate or take joy in the ridicule, and diminishment of others, you will soon encounter a Bigger Billy!

Thus the chapter BILLY GOT BIG!!!!

Tom was having dinner recently with a Middle School teacher, his wife, and two sons. They were discussing the **DPC** *effort to develop a Children's book and our reasoning.*

Both his guest and wife are teachers and began discussing the topic of bullying and its effects on children.

The husband said "ok I have to come clean . . . when I was in second grade I really teased other kids a lot . . . and one of the kids I teased the most was Billy B."

"I never thought of it as cruel and bullying is not how I remember it but I should have realized I was hurting his feelings."

"He did get payback though when we got to Middle School." "I hadn't seen him in a while."

"A few days after we started school a friend came to me and said, 'Bill B. is looking for you . . . and he got big"'!

"I didn't think anything of it . . . until one day I closed my locker and there stood Billy B. and he was huge!" "He started beating on me." "I don't know if I cried, I just wanted to live to First Period."

When he asked, "so what did that teach you . . . and what do you say to your own kids (2024 update now 6'4 and 6'3 and both Black Belts)?"

His response was "well I tell them it is wrong . . . but I also tell them eventually teasers and bully's run into a Billy B. and they will pay." "I tell my 5th Grader's the same story when they lay hands on each other."

As we navigate our futures there are obviously lessons taught for us "older kids", who are in the position to act like "bullies," the best advice we can share is "Beware of Billy"!

Chapter 7
The Constancy of Change

In 1849 the French writer Jean-Baptiste Alphonse Karr wrote "the more things change the more they remain the same."

While the allusion suggests the end result of fluid situations is similarity, the times we are living in suggest a modification to our mental model is in order. Along the lines of it is best not to climb up a tree with no idea as to how climb down!

Two business case areas requiring adaptation are Family Owned/Privately Held Business Succession and Executive Transitions.

Our logic in inserting these two cases into the narrative on leadership is if enterprises tolerate aberrant behaviors their ability to adapt is non-existent. In these two instances there is no margin for error and experimentation is contraindicated.

- Celebration Without The Party

- Executive Transitions 2024

The Celebration Without The Party 2024 Update!

As many of us prepare for change of seasons, **DPC** thought it would be useful to identify a trend that during the Pandemic was somewhat dormant, however now is resurfacing with a vengeance.

Essentially as Boomer, Owner/Founder executives are proactively contemplating their exit from commercial life they are being faced with the dilemma, "what to do with my company"?

The phenomenon **Discussion Partners** began noting almost a decade ago, whereby Succession within the Family-Owned business sector had two dimensions:

1. **Abdication**—family members asserted their desire to engage in career alternatives independent of the "family" business-note this did not encompass forfeiture of inheritance or other forms of economic compensation
2. **Contention**—the HBO series *Succession,* book *Unscripted* and movie *Knives Out* are representative of the declared battles within families when future leadership/beneficiary positions are not carefully constructed and/or there is disagreement with declared wishes

At present **DPC** is working with 11 executives who are wrestling with this dilemma. In addition through affiliation with **The Forever Green Group** based in the UK, cognizant of many European retail firms also dealing with this challenge.

In the 9 years since the publication of this blog, **Discussion Partners** has expanded our involvement with Privately Held/Family-owned businesses to over 500 clients. Succession difficulties now exceeds 70%, and increasing due to workforce attitudes, economics, taxation, gifting, and securing the services of "ready now" executives.

July 2015 Blog

Ask yourself the question what if I invited my family to my birthday party . . . and no one came?

The obvious feelings would be confusion, rejection, hurt, and if a member of my family, a vow of "I'll make them pay"!

Now ask yourself the question . . . "what if I or my parent founded a company, I spent my whole career growing the business with the thought that my children would run it, and they have no interest in doing so"?

Your reactions would likely be similar . . . extended to encompass the parental utterance of "where did I go wrong"?

Fortunately or unfortunately this situation is evolving into a trend that cannot be ignored.

The undeniable facts that surround the reality are as follows:

- The children of owner/founders are oftentimes the beneficiaries of a terrific education

- The children have likely had the opportunity to travel extensively both domestically and internationally

- The children of Boomers have benefitted from the parental conditioning that results in feelings of confidence, experimentation, and encouragement to express oneself

- The children of Boomers are not disposed to think of career decisions in the context of extended tenure . . . more 3 years vs. lifetime in tone and substance

- The children of owner founders are not ungrateful, nor disrespectful, they are looking for different challenges in career progression

There are of course exceptions to this emerging trend. However, the fact that there is an evolving narrative suggests the need to move beyond sentiment towards strategic frameworks.

Executive Transitions 2024—Current Reality

2023 was a pivotal year for executive transitions. The post-Pandemic mentality of "life is too short" led to numerous unanticipated senior level transitions from 2021 through 2023.

Terms such as "The Great Resignation" and "The Great Upgrade" inclusive of senior level incumbents were contributing factors to labor market turbulence. The lack of a major disruption in the Capital Markets allowed for sufficient economic foundation allowing for a "go vs. stay" initiative.

Concomitant to the self-directed decisions of executives to transition, the labor market continues to navigate sub-optimal immigration policies, global recession fears, supply chain concerns, and geo-political dynamics.

As we enter 2024 **DPC** research reinforced by *The Economist, The Atlantic,* **AARP, and McKinsey** *Insights,* suggest the acceleration of executive transitions shows no signs of deceleration.

On the media side the HBO series, **Succession** dramatized the dynamics of this Human Capital process. The book **Unscripted** on the family turmoil associated with a multi-sector *Succession* further suggests many plans are more fiction than fact. The net result is further turmoil in the executive cohort IF departures are un-planned, or absent continuity scenarios, chaos is a likely outcome.

Our 2024 working hypothesis is: *"Plan For The Worst-Hope For The Best While Curbing Your Optimism"* The refrain "I can't find enough people to grow my company" will not diminish this year and will continue to be complicated by executive transitions.

Over the past the last three years in Discussion Partner's Transition Advisory work in the Privately Held/Family Owned business sector (167 clients), we have found in 67% of circumstances there has not been a passing along of the business to the next generation of family members.

Notwithstanding the disappointment that is unavoidable, quickly the parent realizes in fact it is a tribute as their children are manifesting a "mind of their own."

The "top 5" considerations as the owner transitions to the next steps encompass:

- **Estate Planning**—development of a comprehensive plan that provides reassurance that wealth creation for the family has been secured

- **Timing Determination**—the senior leader then has to determine how long they choose to stay involved. In our experience unless there are detracting circumstances, this is likely to be approximately 3 years

- **Growth Acceleration**—we oftentimes the executive has a new found energy and concomitant with their now extended tenure, focus on innovative strategic intents inclusive of new processes, products, and geographies.

- **Transaction Contemplation**—independent of potential buyer, employee, strategic, or investor driven, the executive focuses on a troika of refined initiatives inclusive of a) cleaning up of the balance sheet, b) raising the bar on performance, and c) replenishment of leadership population, as all are transaction enhancers.

The "now what" is understandable, the "where did I go wrong" assumption, is not appropriate as you are by no means alone AND the fact that you raised independent children is a tribute.

What is necessary is a purpose-built framework that predicts an alternative future for the company concomitant with an attitude of "enjoy the ride"!

Discussion Partners Research -Labor Market & Executive Aspirations

The above is supported by **Discussion Partners** research and client involvement. Beginning in April 2020, we identified a likely post-Pandemic trend where many executives would begin self-selecting accelerated transitions from their leadership roles.

This phenomenon continued through 2023 and our prediction is will remain in force this year.

DPC identified an urgent initiative should be the reconstitution of High Potential Development programs. **Discussion Partners** recommendations were highlighted in our June 2020 book, *Leadership Development-The Next Curve to Flatten!*

The Covid-19 Pandemic was a game changer, which continues into 2024 for executives who approach their careers with an attitude of: "Life is too short or I have other interests I want to pursue." We are also finding that executives, if not leaving immediately, are adopting what **DPC** refers to as "the Divisibility Factor"–i.e., dividing by two their original departure date.

Discussion Partners identified an approach that we actively encourage be considered for 2024 as enterprises navigate executive transitions.

1. Frame the challenge in terms of strategic, leadership and demographically realistic terms.

2. Embrace the reality that hybrid is here to stay and create a dashboard that monitors vs. tries to disprove the concept.

3. Do neither by design nor inference manifest a lack of career commitment to those who prefer a hybrid model.

4. Do a reset of leadership development programs emphasizing empathy, transparency, collaboration, and predictability skills development.

5. Create soft-landing company affiliation programs for executives who choose to transition through advisory, mentoring, emeritus approaches.

6. Clear delineation of who is and isn't a high potential while insuring the commitment for development of the franchise players.

7. Isolate while tolerating leaders who "don't get it," transitioning them to "first do no harm" circumstances.

8. Re-examine Total Rewards strategy for diversity, equity, and inclusion.

9. Adopt the Roosevelt adage for recruitment: "Try everything. If it works, keep doing it. If not, try something else."

10. Assume your company is a learning laboratory—develop aggressively.

The demographic realities with broader context of *aspirational* and *attitudinal* influencers suggest it is contraindicated not to think situational vs. traditional, as the problem is not a short-lived dilemma, but rather a systemic challenge that will be with us for a while.

Executive Transitions—The 2024 Prediction

As referenced in **Discussion Partners** two books on transitions, in the not-so-distant past, there was something magical about age 65 as it was when most left the workforce. At the time, however, after they received their gold watch and embarked on a cruise, there was not much life left based upon actuarial tables and cultural norms.

The last 20 years have seen a dynamic change in date certain for transitions in the context of the mantra, "It is time to retire retirement," captured in the book *Workforce Crisis* by Ken Dychtwald, Tammy Erickson, and Bob Morison reinforced by thought leaders Doctors Lynda Gratton and Andrew Scott in their books, *The 100 Year Life* and *The Next Long Life*, focusing on favorable demographics. Also in the recent past, Tom Wilson's *Next Stage* and Ken Dychtwald and Bob Morison's *What Retirees Want* concentrating on transition planning were published all with the similar thematic: *The demographics being addressed by arcane attitudes and policies are the most problematic of enterprise challenges.*

Chip Conley, the best selling author and co-founder of The Modern Elder Academy in his just published book ***Learning To Love Midlife*** reinforces age driven aspirations, inclusive of executives, to be proactive in pursuit of life experience. This book adds to the phenomenon **DPC** noted in 2020 whereby executives are accelerating their retirement plans in pursuit of non-job related fulfillment experiences.

Discussion Partner Collaborative Executive Transition Experience

Discussion Partners launched a Transition Advisory Service offering in 2013 after the publication of our book, *Executive Transitions-Plotting the Opportunity!*

Since that time, we have worked with over 900 executives in a variety of sectors and published now two best selling books on the topic most recently *Executive Transitions 2-Leveraging Experience for Future Success!*

In respect to our experience, we have organized our **Transition Advisory** support into four phases.

Phase 1-Ensuring Enterprise Continuity making sure that care and thought are given to the preservation of momentum as manifested in the Succession Plan through constructive access, advice, and prescriptive documentation.

Interim Period Issues—Post Successor Selection

Be mindful there is oftentimes a "rock in the middle of the river" attitude to be avoided in a post-announcement environment. Be advised we usually find "the obstruction" well intentioned and focused on the executives "best interests" so as "not to bother them." Still, it is difficult to be working in an environment that seems to have forgotten one has a pulse.

While there WILL be a feeling of emotional disorientation associated with departure, it is most advisable to recognize that **Transition** is a platform to other areas of personal and creative expression and by no means the suspension of commercial and personal interests.

The Playbook

The suggestion of this exercise may seem odd. However, our experience is that it is *particularly* useful when a Successor may not be up to the task immediately. It is also nontrivial in reaffirmation of legacy.

The value of having a brief treatise on your experience with a limited distribution is twofold:

a) Helps others see "your role through your eyes" and

b) Reduces "blowback" in that after you leave, it's less likely you'd be blamed for others' mistakes.

Our concept is a 2- to 3-page memorandum, which focuses on the following:

- The initiatives that you feel were well executed;

- Those that are in process and/or you feel were deficient;

- Two to three top-of-mind suggestions for securing progress in your previous role.

Phase 2-Legacy Driven Next Stage Launch - Succinctly put, it's taking proactive steps to ensure that the efforts you undertook and the success you engendered are recalled in the most positive terms as you embark on your "next stage."

In **Discussion Partners'** experience regardless of age and psychographic profile, it is prudent to substitute the question of: "How will I focus my energies for the next three to five years?" to: "What will I do with the rest of my life?" This is the principle of **Inflection Point, which** we utilize in our discussions with executives who have an extensive work history often with one to two employers.

Transition Principles

The below represents a baseline from which we develop tactics for executives who are departing from a "continuing concern."

✓ **Control the Communication Process**—Avoid relying only on the formal elements of communication. There is a need to augment this effort with an informal communication process to personalize and engage in conversations with selected managers.

✓ **Confirm the Legacy**—There is a need to define "how I want to be remembered" from "how I am perceived." The most effective way to do this is to have a dialogue with trusted advisors where you pointblank ask the question: "What will you remember about me?"

✓ **Networking**—Classify your internal and external networks capturing the contact information for managers who would provide insight/access for you in the future—what we refer to as the "Nifty 50." This is the minimum! There is a need to commit to interacting with these folks at least on a quarterly basis, recognizing that the interactions will be sustainable provided the dialogue has mutual value.

✓ **Relationship Sustainability**—The first order of business is to prepare and send, following the formal announcement, an e-mail to at least these 50 executives internal and external embedded with: a) preliminary thoughts as to career focus and b) contact information.

✓ **Accessibility**—Independent of the networking activity above, there is a need to utilize multiple vehicles (e-mails, social media, and the lost art of letter writing) to maintain contact with a broader number of executives.

Phase 3 - Rejuvenation Break - Taking a break to recharge and reflect on next steps in your career trajectory.

The Concept of the Commercial Sabbatical

The foundation for the "Commercial Sabbatical" concept we promote derives from our research and client experience. Based upon executive demographics and aspirations, it is embedded within our hypothesis that successful executives after a period of disconnection are desirous to reengage in commercial activities.

1. **Older Executives (65 plus)** focus on two or three activities part time post-transition.

2. **Bridge Executives (55 to 65)** focus on two or three activities part time post-transition for a period of approximately two years then return to "work" in an advisory and/or employee capacity at a level of approximately 50% of the time until age 65 or older.

3. **Off-Ramp/On-Ramp Executives (55 and below) if not focused on replication of a full-time setting immediately** focus on two to three activities for a period of approximately one year and then return to work as advisors and/or employees until age 65 at a level in excess of 50%.

Phase 4 - Cyclical Planning - Conceptualization, deliberation, and implementation of the plan developed prior to departure and refined subsequently.

A critical finding from **DPC** experience to date is executives have an attitude that control of calendar is the primary filter for determinant as to where and how they will be spending their time.

Transitioning Executive Research

The below represents our current thinking on the question: "Where are executives likely to spend their time post-employment?" Our assumptions are derived from our initial research project of over 2,000 executives, ongoing pulse surveys since 2013 and our transition advisory work with over 800 executive clients.

Be advised our overarching finding is that while it is likely executives will engage in two or three endeavors part time as aforementioned, there is a manifested desire to "control the calendar."

<u>Discussion Partner Transition Focus</u>

- **New Role/Alternative Employer**
- **Consulting Advisory**
- **Academic Pursuit as Adjunct Professor**
- **Author/Blogger**
- **Personal Investor**
- **Commercial Board Membership**
- **Political Involvement**
- **Philanthropy**
- **Social Responsibility (including NGO Boards)**
- **Higher Education-Student**

- **Arts**

- **Entrepreneur—non-commercial**

- **Start-Up Initiator**

- **Sports – Recreational**

- **Other - Rock Star?**

Discussion Partners Transition Advisory Conclusions

Over a decade ago, Tammy Erickson, Ken Dychtwald and Bob Morison in their McKinsey award-winning *HBR* article, "*It's Time to Retire Retirement*" and their follow-up book *Workforce Crisis* asserted in an elegant way that retirement is not a phase down from relevance. Moreover, it is a platform for one to pursue alternative interests and avenues for personal satisfaction—points of view borne out by **DPC** research and client experience.

Discussion Partners' research and advisory interdictions reinforce this hypothesis. Moreover, as we enter 2024, the shift in demographics with the now largest worker cohort (Millennial and Gen Z born before 2002), global economic dynamics, the whole arena of executive transitions is at a crossroads.

The three requisites **Discussion Partners** encourages are:

1) Enterprise support to executives in conceptualizing their personal plan.

2) Rigorous analysis as to the readiness of the successor.

3) A shift in attitude on the part of the executive to embark on the beginning of new adventures, not an end of relevance and contribution.

The Labor Shortage complicated by the Great Resignations should prompt a sense of urgency and experimentation in all Talent Readiness areas, particularly Executive Transitions.

Chapter 8

Closing Observations & The Precedent of History

As we near November it is not an exaggeration to say the eyes of the world are focused on the US Presidential election.

The elongated political campaign can realistically be portrayed as having begun in November 2020 when the results of that election began being disputed.

Events such as January 6th, 100+ lawsuits contributing to a rapid decline in faith in judicial institutions, pronounced polarization and acrimony in the political arena lead many domestic and international **DPC** clients to venture 2 questions:

- Has it ever been this bad?

- Will normalcy prevail post election?

Addressing question 2 first, normalcy may be more wistful memory and exaggerated in respect to positive reminiscing.

As it relates to question 1, **DPC** began engaging in a series of Pulse Survey's, and Focus groups to identify turbulent events where there was an "All is Lost" concern.

More importantly to engender a point of view based on precedent, that chaos is not new, and **history indicates that optimism is not misplaced.**

During our search for "precedents" the one deemed by a vote within the **DPC** community were the events leading up to the US Civil War.

Historians dispute this events root cause as due to slavery, states rights, or economic vibrancy? What are inarguable are the parallels to today's chaos.

In 1820 The Missouri Compromise allowed for the admission of Missouri as a "slave state", and Maine as a "free state."

In 1857 the Dred Scott decision declared it illegal for Congress to abolish slavery while a) challenging the constitutionality of The Missouri Compromise, b) declaring even free persons of color could not enjoy the benefits of citizenship.

The SJC's decision appeared to be politically biased given the southern geographic origins of Justices.

The election of Lincoln in 1860 provided an impetus to declaring loyalty. Confederate General Robert E. Lee, was initially considered for the position of Union Army leader, Jefferson Davis was a US Senator later Confederacy President, and John Breckenridge was US Vice President and later went on to be CSA Secretary of War.

The confluence of circumstances being similar to US current reality compelled **DPC** to suspend the collection of feedback at **1860** for symbolic reasons.

Among our clients, research population and within the **DPC** community while many have strongly held political views on both sides of the spectrum, the shared position is revulsion with the tone of discourse and hypocritical behaviors.

As stipulated in our Introduction **Discussion Partners** 2021 research into desired leadership behaviors post Pandemic was unambiguous in identifying the top 4 as follows:

1. **Empathy**

2. **Transparency**

3. **Accountability &**

4. **Collaboration**

The research for this book allowed for similar clarity regarding those "reprehensible" behaviors our respondents believe to be the least attractive in a leader:

1. **Hypocrisy**

2. **Bias**

3. **Intolerance**

4. **Expediency &**

5. **Aggressiveness**

Candidly we have been struggling with a way to end this opus utilizing a positive real life example.

Fortunately, Tom's nephew, Sean Casey, a 20-year Army veteran and communications professional at **Comcast**, led several strategic communications initiatives supporting the **Xfinity** brand's *"The Aviators"* advertising campaign.

The ad, centered around four Vietnam-era military aviators played by real Vietnam veterans, was an outstanding collaboration between teams across **Comcast NBCUniversal** and external partners. The initiative went far beyond promoting a product; it reinforced the value of connection, camaraderie, and respect.

This dynamic project, impacting everything from marketing to customer service, reminds us that a leader is defined by actions, not rhetoric, and that collaboration is not just a word; it is an aspiration.

Sean was one of the key collaborators. A significant outcome was the feedback from the profiled pilots who served during an unpopular war.

"I never expected to be treated with such dignity, respect, and care."

In our discussions, Sean pointed out two interconnected leadership values. First, Leading Through Influence, a component of the commercial effort. Second, the military model of Commander's End State, essentially an envisioned future that allows for adaptation. He felt that both inputs led to a widely heralded outcome for "The Aviators" campaign.

Integrating this example with the five years of research undertaken by **Discussion Partners**, encompassing over 3000 inputs, we strongly recommend pivoting from the abstract to the tactical.

Leadership requires ongoing self-assessment and refinement of behaviors to enhance the positive and eradicate the negative.

In closing our research has led **DPC** to crave December 2024 as the transition to replace chaos with clarity, reduce rhetoric, while enjoining in more focused discussions of beneficial leadership attributes that are respected.

Leaders wherever they sit have an obligation to exhibit behaviors that inspire trust and respect, as any less of a commitment only complicates the already challenging dynamics.

Again quoting Prime Minister Thatcher to provoke reflection . . .

"One can always get lucky, the question is can you remain always lucky."

Other Books by Tom Casey

INFLECTION POINTS
The Career Guide
for Pursuing Opportunities while Ignoring Restraints!
Tom Casey
Sean Casey
with
Ariana Pazos Aramburú

TALENT READINESS
THE FUTURE IS NOW
Leading a
Multi-Generational Workforce
BY
TOM CASEY
with TIM DONAHUE and ERIC SEUBERT

EXECUTIVE TRANSITIONS
A Guide for Transitioning Executives and the Companies that Employ Them
Tom Casey and Karen Wartin
with
Sean Casey and Tobey Choate

EXECUTIVE ADVICE TO THE YOUNG
Don't Repeat My Mistakes!
Tom Casey & Gino Piaggio Valdez
with
Tobey Choate, Catherine Chase Heilman, Casey Lawlor Osborne,
Tricia Lawlor Jordan, Ada Zuric & Jody Galdzle Reamer

EXECUTIVE TRANSITIONS 2
Leveraging Experience
For Future Success!
FUTURE SUCCESS
TRANSITIONS
LEVERAGE
EXPERIENCE
Thomas F. Casey Jr.

LEADERSHIP DEVELOPMENT
The Next Curve to Flatten
Tom Casey and Claire Hebert-Dow
with
Deborah Hicks and Gino Piaggio Valdez

About the Authors

Thomas F. Casey, Jr.

Tom Casey is the Founder and Managing Principal of **Discussion Partner Collaborative**, a Research Consultancy with over 200 Advisors in 21 global locations.

He is the author of over 800 articles, blogs, and 6 books on leadership 5 of which have been recognized as "best sellers" most recently *Leadership Development-The Next Curve To Flatten!*

During his near five decades of Consulting experience he has worked with firms such as **PwC, Arthur D. Little, Harbridge House,** and **The Concours Group** before founding **Discussion Partners.**

Tom is a graduate of the **University of Alaska**, holds **MA** and **MBA** degrees from **Rivier University,** and the Executive Program at **Yale University.**

Tom is both a **United States Air Force** and **Army** Special Operations Veteran. He retired from the Army Reserve as a Colonel.

Tom can be reached at: tcasey@dpcadvisors.com

Claire Hebert-Dow

A lifelong resident of the Lakes Region in New Hampshire, Ms. Hebert-Dow never successful in curing herself of the wanderlust affixed to her imagination. First picturing herself as a French interpreter at the U.N. followed by a desire to earn a Psychology degree and spend a lifetime working through solutions for everybody else's issues, she would settle for writing a memoir through the eyes of her five cats and one dog. She credits a **BA** in Psychology and a **MA** in creative writing, Non Fiction for giving her the tools to complete *Saving Mama*—*set* to launch Fall, 2024. Beginning five years ago she began working with Tom Casey co-authoring blogs and the best selling business book, ***Leadership Development-The Next Curve To Flatten!***

Claire can be reached at: clairehebert8@icloud.com

Other Contributors

Elizabeth Freudmann

Elizabeth (better known as Lizy) Freudmann is a marketing strategist with a special interest in behavioral economics. She has worked with a range of businesses throughout her career, from top 40 musicians to financial service institutions. Clients have included startups and solopreneurs, academic institutions and brick-and-mortar shops. Lizy loves marketing because she loves connecting with people. She earned her **BA** in American Civilization (yes, that is a thing!) from Brown University, and both her **MBA** and **Masters** in Global Business from Tulane University. She lives in New Orleans, and her company, One More Thing was the first Certified B Corp in the state of Louisiana.

Lizy can be reached at: lizy@onemorethingllc.com

Sean Casey

Sean Casey is a strategic communications professional and U.S. Army Reserve officer with over twenty years of military service, including two tours to Iraq. Presently, he is the Senior Director of Communications at **Comcast NBCUniversal**, concentrating on Military Engagement programs. He was involved in the company's "The Aviators" short film and advertising campaign, which recognized the impact of Internet connectivity on the lifelong bonds among veterans. He holds a **Bachelor's** degree in Political Science from Miami University and a **Master's** in Public Communications from Drexel University. He's a contributor to several of Tom

Casey's books and his co-author on the best selling book *Inflection Points—The Career Guide for Pursuing Opportunities while Ignoring Restraints!*

Sean can be reached at: caseysb42@gmail.com